Innovation by Creativity

Fifty-one tools for solving problems creatively

Max van Leeuwen
Hans Terhürne

Innovation by creativity

By Max van Leeuwen and Hans Turhürne

Copyright © 2009

Cover Design By Happyhopscotch (www.happyhopscotch.com)

Book Design and Typesetting by Happyhopscotch

Set in Bliss 12 on 18pt

First published in 2010 by:

Ecademy Press

6 Woodland Rise, Penryn, Cornwall TR10 8QD, UK

info@ecademy-press.com   www.ecademy-press.com

Printed and Bound by:

Lightning Source in the UK and USA

Printed on acid-free paper from managed forests. This book is printed on demand, so no copies will be remaindered or pulped.

ISBN-978-1-905823-72-7

INNOVATION BY CREATIVITY

The utmost care has been taken with this publication. Nevertheless the authors accept no liability for information that is incomplete or incorrect. They will be pleased to accept any recommendations with regard to improvements.

Illustrations Chapter 4: Cees Willemse

CONTENTS

1. INTRODUCTION

Why creativity?

Ever more often, creative solutions are sought for the problems, big or small, with which we are confronted on a daily basis. Sometimes because we cannot find a logical solution, sometimes because a creative solution is needed because of commercial considerations and sometimes because we are not satisfied with the logical solution.

Many companies are undergoing changes that place new demands on their staff. The need to use and stimulate the creativity of employees is often brought up during management training. Developments in our society require creativity in large measures.

What is creativity?

A creative person looks the same as anyone else but thinks differently. Creativity is multifaceted. One of the definitions of creativity talks about the ability to combine existing things in different ways in order to end up with something new. By combining the wine press and the matrix, Gutenberg arrived at the idea of the printing press. Another way of looking at creativity is to play with the mutual associations between things. Creativity is the ability to generate new and useful ideas and solutions for everyday problems and challenges. The more we load the definition of creativity with values, opinions and symbols, the more we limit creativity. The more we address ourselves as to how these values, opinions and symbols are formed, the better the chance that creativity will be less fettered.

How do I become more creative?
The simplest answer is: "Go for a walk". How many ideas have you not had while you were out walking, cycling, driving your car or doing the dishes? The brain continuously receives stimulation and continuously produces ideas. A good technique is to work on a problem just before you go to sleep. Your subconscious takes over while you sleep. Evaluate the ideas when you wake up.

Everyone has the potential to be creative. Every one of us can create something. Only not everyone is aware of this. Creative people seem to be able to home in on their thought patterns and in this way gather good ideas. People who do not use their creative potential either do not know how to do this or are not aware of the possibilities. Creative people are able to think something over and then to forget about it. Meanwhile the thinking process continues unconsciously. Later the conscious thinking process is again resumed and the brain has unconsciously produced some ideas.

In order to become more creative you have to have the right qualities, be motivated and have the opportunity to actually produce something creative. The first thing you have to do to become more creative is to give yourself permission to do

things in a creative way. The second is to conquer your personal
barriers.

A few things that will help you to heighten your creativity:

- read books on creativity techniques
- do a course on creative thinking
- keep a diary of your ideas, thoughts, etc. and read it regularly
- relax regularly and take sufficient time off for leisure
- develop an interest in various things, preferably things that have nothing to do with your day-to-day work
- do not work too hard (it takes time to distance yourself after a period of being intensively preoccupied with a problem)

Creativity is not a gift. It is an attitude. This book provides you with a number of tools that will help you, but it will not automatically change your ideas about yourself or your creativity. You will have to do that for yourself. Everyone can do it, everyone has got what it takes!

A program to further your creativity should include the following steps:

1. Formulate measurable goals, e.g.:

- generate 15% more solutions within 6 months
- find a solution to problem X within 2 weeks

• generate ideas using brainstorming (come up with at least 100 ideas for a new pen)

2. Formulate criteria to establish whether you have achieved the goals, e.g.:

- the ideas are new
- the ideas are useful, solve the problem or meet the requirement
- the ideas can be implemented within the required time and the available budget.

3. Read and learn about creativity techniques.

4. Create an environment for yourself with people you trust and respect.

5. Celebrate your successes.

6. Look upon yourself as a creative person.

How do you restrain creativity?

Creativity is often hindered by the following obstacles:

- working too hard and too intensively on a problem
- objectives that contradict one another
- giving yourself too little opportunity to relax.

Most of the time the obstacles are of your own making:

- being afraid of criticism
- lacking in self-confidence
- your physical and mental condition

Environmental factors can also play a part:

- a sterile environment that does not stimulate the senses
- the need for short-term results
- rules that prevent us from gathering information, perhaps together with others.

Other factors that stand in the way of handling things creatively:

- stress
- routine work
- sticking to existing viewpoints
- anxiety
- self-criticism.

What do we want to achieve with this book?
We are not trying to reinvent the wheel. What we want to do is to provide you with a few tools in an accessible way. We have purposely not included some difficult tools and we have limited the amount of detail we go into with some of the tools.

In the first instance, use those techniques which appeal to you most. Experiment with them but bear the order of the various steps in mind (see chapter 4: "Frame for a Creative Thought Process"). We are sure that when you use the creativity techniques you will find that solving the problems with which you are confronted will become easier, quicker and more pleasurable.

Max van Leeuwen
Hans Terhürne

2. COMMUNICATION

Wherever people work together they also communicate. Communication is simply the sending and receiving of messages. Generally this does not cause too many problems, but breakdowns can often occur between the sender and the receiver. Communication takes place in many different ways. We mainly use it on a conscious level; we talk to each other, we read books, look at pictures or watch television and in doing so, we send or receive information.

People also communicate with each other during creativity sessions. We try to give and receive information in different ways. During these sessions there are a number of different aspects of communication that deserve further attention. These aspects can be divided into two groups, i.e.:

- Making conscious use of a kind of breakdown in communication, i.e. differences in interpretation;
- Prevention of real breakdowns in communication.

These points are explained in more detail below.

We use creativity and apply it in our methods to try to create new, original thoughts, ideas and solutions that can help us to solve our problems. For this purpose we make use of the human brain's ability to associate, to get from one thought to another, without any apparent logical link between them.
If we examine the flow of ideas during a session more closely, we

perceive what we call "turning points". These are associations brought about by a different interpretation of a concept. For example, one of the participants says the word "buck" (meaning the animal) and someone else comes up with another association in which the word "buck" is understood as meaning a dollar.

Facilitators as well as participants can make use of this. Recognizing, seeking and stressing these concepts stimulates creativity.

Making use of differences in interpretation provides the opportunity to stimulate creativity. It is also very important to prevent actual breakdowns in communication during sessions. A number of aspects of a good mutual exchange of information are explained below.

- Listening

The receiving of information is necessary for the proper understanding of the messages from the other participants. It is normal for these messages to bring your own flow of thoughts into action (by association etc.) and to be derived from the story being told. A simple aid to help you to keep concentrating on the speaker is the interim noting down of thoughts by the receiver, so your attention can once more be turned towards the person telling the story.

- Body language

The body is also a sender of information. It is important for both the sender and the receiver that the message being sent is supported by the language spoken by the body. The physical signals that someone sends out can be perceived and reacted to if necessary. Disinterest, embarrassment, restlessness, anger, joy, etc. are often clearly manifested. It is primarily up to the facilitator to react to this and to lead the process in a desirable direction.

- Giving everyone a chance

Very often communication breaks down because each participant is caught up in his/her own thought flow and wants to communicate these thoughts to the whole group. As a result group discussions often turn into (violent) discussions in which only one's own opinion appears to be of importance.

In group discussions it is important to arrive at a dialogue instead of a discussion. A good aid for this is to collectively agree that every participant waits 5 seconds before reacting after the previous speaker has finished. You can then be sure the previous speaker has definitely finished, and you can take time to collect your thoughts and not overreact.

There are of course many other issues of importance to participants in creativity sessions as far as communication is concerned. The points mentioned here are only a small aid to improving the quality of the sessions. However, this is as far as we can go in this book; further reading, practicing and getting experience are the best ways of mastering creative thinking. A number of aspects which are of particular importance to the facilitator are discussed in more detail in the next chapter.

3. FACILITATION

Many of the methods discussed in this book are applied in groups. This means that someone will have to lead the group process. We call this person the facilitator.

Although facilitation is an important element in the application of creativity methods in groups, this book should not be viewed as a manual for facilitators.

However, we have set out a number of points that can be important. There is a wide range of courses and training sessions on leading group discussions on offer.

Facilitation can be easily divided into three phases, viz. the preparation, the session and the conclusion. Each phase consists of a number of different aspects.

Preparation

First of all the facilitator must have a clear picture of what the principal wants. The "assignment process" can be supplemented in different ways but it is essential that the assignment is clear and simple. For the organization and implementation of the creativity session, the problem definition should also be clear to the principal and the facilitator.

In preparation of the session, a number of practical matters such as a location and materials should first be arranged in order to ensure that the session can be properly implemented. When choosing a location, the following points, amongst others, should be taken into account:

- the size of the location and its accessibility (if possible a location that is new and unfamiliar to the participants);
- a room that is inspiring and certainly not distracting;
- no interruptions (e.g. no mobile phones);
- the ability to be able to fix papers to the wall.

Materials required to properly implement the session include:

- pens, paper;
- marker pens, flip charts;
- stickers in various colors;

Some other materials or equipment may be necessary depending on the method(s) to be used. Always make sure that these things are ready so that no time is wasted during the session.

As the facilitator you must make a decision before the session as to the method to be used for the problem at hand. Let yourself be guided by the problem definition (the type of problem), your own experience (which methods suit you best) and the composition of the group (does the group have experience in creativity or not). Naturally the composition of the group is determined in consultation with the principal and the participants are invited and given a rough idea as to what is expected of them.

As the facilitator, draw up a schedule for the meeting and set out the main points on paper. A big piece of paper with the schedule on it fixed to the wall during the session enables participants to

see which point in the program they are working on. Hanging up
an enlarged copy of the rules of play is also a good aid.

It is important to begin and end the session at the agreed times.

Rules of play
During the creative part of the session special rules of play apply;
these are listed and explained below. The facilitator will have to
explain these clearly and indicate during the session when these
rules apply.

1. Deferment of verdict
When the participants generate ideas and potential solutions,
it is not intended that other participants pass judgment on
these ideas. Random comments that detract from the ideas
mentioned are also absolutely forbidden.

2. Lying permissible
You do not always have to speak the truth during the creativity
session. Impossibilities, contradictions and untruths may be used
as long as they do not endanger the process and so long as no
factual inaccuracies remain after the session (the use of untruths
to find potential new solutions can be valuable).

3. Privacy externally and openness internally
You can impart confidential information during the session.
There should in fact be a large measure of openness amongst
the participants. In this regard all participants will have to be
certain in the knowledge that what is discussed in the meeting
will definitely not be taken outside of it. What can be taken
outside are the results, not the intrinsic process.

4. Extra attention to naive questions and comments
What are often thought of as stupid questions and suggestions can make participants think about self-evident facts and presuppositions, opening up new directions for thought and deviating from the accepted route.

5. No hierarchy and no arrogance
During the session everyone is equal and the same input is expected from all. All ideas and comments are of equal value and not weighted according to the position of the originator. The participants must be confident that they will not be called to account subsequently for specific remarks they may have made during the meeting.

6. A critical phase afterwards
As indicated in chapter 4 ('Frame for a Creative Process'), a critical phase should always follow a creativity session. By doing this all the ideas from this phase start to take on a life of their own.

Implementation
The session is always conducted according to the scheme set out in chapter 4. In the schedule this is translated into the specific circumstances of the problem definition and those of the participants.

There are nevertheless a number of aspects of the scheme that require further explanation.

• In order to ensure that the session gets off to a good start it is very important to translate the right information on the problem definition into a reformulation so that all participants have a good and clear understanding of the problem. The facilitator plays a very important role in this section; he must be able to ensure that the group arrives at an acceptable reformulation. An important aid in this phase is paraphrasing or the reiteration of information in your own words, which prompts the question as to whether this translated information clearly indicates what is meant.

- The facilitator has drawn up a schedule for the session and has chosen a number of methods. However, it sometimes happens that (some of) the participants and the facilitator meet for the first time at the session. The session leader must then assess whether the chosen methods are valid or whether they suit the group. It will often also be necessary to break through or weaken the resistance to the application of the creativity methods. One of the ways to do this is to use warm-ups, short exercises as examples of creative thinking. This book contains a number of these warm-ups.

- The participants are partly determined by the facilitator in the preparatory discussions with the principal. Attention is paid to this during the preparatory phase. The participants assume various roles during the session. The roles which always recur, are listed below with a short explanation.

- The problem owner is the person (or a representative or a group/organization/company with a problem) whose problem is discussed during the session. The problem owner will give an explanation of the problem definition at the start of the meeting. He/she also actively participates in the rest of the session. In the critical phase this person can also be given another task, viz. the critical evaluation of the ideas generated and perhaps even the choice of ideas to be elaborated upon.

- The facilitator (session leader) is responsible for ensuring that the meeting runs smoothly. He/she will not be concerned with the content of the problem definition and the generation of ideas.
- The secretary is the person who notes down what is said during the entire session. Depending on the size of the group, the problem and the method(s) chosen, this function can be undertaken by a separate person or by the facilitator him/herself.
- The other participants can also be problem owners, employees or participants from outside the organization. The participating group can be composed of people who have a general knowledge of the problem (generalists), people who have a specific (expert) knowledge of the problem (specialists) and people who on the whole have no relationship with the problem (outsiders). A diverse group provides greater variety in respect of ideas and potential for solutions.

The facilitator must make it clear at the start of the meeting what the participants' roles are and what is expected of them. It must also be clear during the session what point in the process the participants have arrived at; this should also be specified from time to time.

Conclusion

As is clearly indicated in chapter 4 ("Frame for a Creative Process"), the session must always be rounded off with a critical phase and a final conclusion. These must also give a clear indication of how to continue dealing with the problem and the solutions found. These form the beginning of a subsequent phase in which the solution is implemented in a specific manner.

As the process guide, the facilitator is responsible for completing this phase and must therefore clearly indicate to the group where the session ends and where the subsequent phase begins. Only once that has been done can the session be regarded as a completed whole.

4. FRAME FOR A CREATIVE PROCESS

The creative process can be sub-divided into a number of phases. The Center for the Development of Creative Thinking (COCD) uses the Problem Development, Idea Development and Idea Evaluation phases. These phases can be sub-divided into ten different stages:

problem definition
- stage 1: formulation of problem
- stage 2: acceptance
- stage 3: re-formulation

idea development
- stage 4: analysis and purge (attempt to find logical solutions)
- stage 5: exhaustion, frustration
- stage 6: relaxation/incubation
- stage 7: creative side step
- stage 8: eureka!

idea evaluation
- stage 9: elaboration (critical phase)
- stage 10: plan of action

Stage 1. Problem formulation

The "problem owner" provides information about the problem. It is important that the problem owner is competent and involved and is ultimately in a position to do something about it. During this stage,

clarification questions can be asked (who, what, where, when, why, how?) but the problem is not discussed as yet. Even if the approach is an individual one, it is a good thing to first make a brief note of the most important facts. The important issue here is "the problem as given". Criteria can also be put forward which the ultimate solution will have to meet. Do not allow more than a quarter of an hour for problem formulation.

Stage 2. Acceptance of the problem
The problem or issue is taken over by the group. The problem is now <u>your</u> problem.

Stage 3. Reformulation of the problem
We often look for answers to the wrong question. In that case we have usually formulated the actual problem badly or clumsily. The initial formulation, compiled by the problem owner, places the problem in a very specific light. By looking at the problem from as many different angles as possible, you increase the involvement of the participants, and the problem owner will probably also see his own problem from a different angle. If necessary, specify the criteria which the ultimate solution will have to meet.

Stage 4. Logical analysis and purge (attempt to find logical solutions)

Collect information relating to the issue or the definition of the problem. Analyze the situation and/or any (underlying) processes, look at what the possible causes of a problem might be (and in doing so avoid treating the symptoms). Collect as many ideas and potential solutions as possible.

Stage 5. Exhaustion, frustration

Continue collecting ideas and potential solutions until you are exhausted and perhaps even frustrated.

You might already have found excellent solutions which comply fully with the specified criteria. Work on these and skip to stage 9.

Stage 6. Putting the problem out of your head (relaxation, incubation)

Distance yourself from the problem and direct your attention to other matters for a while. Take a walk (but do take a notebook and pen with you!) or sleep on it overnight. You will continue to work on the issue or the problem subconsciously.

During the session (no time for a night's sleep!), making time for a short, light-hearted brainstorming session or some other form of warm-up can have an incubating effect and can help to prepare you for the next stage. This can also free you from established thought patterns.

Stage 7. Creative side step (intervention of a catalyst)

This is the core of the creative process: the "creative initiative". Tackle this stage with as much input of skills in the field of association, perception and imagination as possible. Take the rules of play for creative thinking into account and make use of one or more techniques. The various techniques all have their own scenarios and are set out in the following section along with the analysis and evaluation techniques.

All ideas and potential solutions which result from the side step are added to the list from the purge phase (stage 4).

Stage 8. Eureka!

Suddenly a connection will be made between what is happening or has happened during the creative side step and the actual problem. The brilliant idea or a number of good solutions are there.

28 Stage 9. Elaborating on the ideas (critical phase)

Make a critical evaluation of the ideas and solutions generated during the first brainstorming session in stage 4 and the creative side step in stages 6/7. Divide them into clusters, select the most promising ideas and test them against the criteria specified in stages 1, 3 and/or 9.

Stage 10. Plan of action

Test the solution found and refine it where necessary. Finally, draw up a final report with a plan of action.

The creative process is a total process in which this order is often not strictly adhered to. Some phases may overlap, or the process might evolve in a series of circles. The important issue here is the basic principle of the creative process, which you can deviate from if you think it is necessary.

5. THE TOOL SELECTOR

A number of different methods can be used in the stages of the
creativity process set out in the previous chapter. Also known as
tools, these methods are dealt with individually later on in this
book. These tools have been developed for one or more stages
of the creative process. The stage(s) for which the tools are used
are also described below.

To be able to put together a program for a complete creative
process, it is necessary to select several tools so that all stages in
the process can be implemented. An overview with all the tools
and the stages for which they are suitable is a handy aid. The
tool selector is intended for this purpose.

The table on the next page has a list of all the tools in the left-
hand column plus the various stages (from 1 to 10) for which
they are suitable or intended across the top. The order of the
tools in the selector agrees with the order of the descriptions of
the tools further on in this book.

There are no specific criteria for selecting the various tools in a
program for a complete creative process. However there are a
number of aspects which may help you make your choice.

Size of group
The size of group for which the tool is suitable is indicated for
each tool. This may help simplify the choice.

Requisites

The materials needed as a very minimum for each tool are specified. This can also influence the choice of tool.

Coordination

Coordination is desirable for combinations of tools from different process stages. The tools must fit together to a certain extent. The descriptions of the tools indicate whether they fit together or not in relation to, for example, the time taken, the degree of difficulty or the resources needed. A very large number of combinations is possible.

Experience

When trying out the various tools, your own experience will increase. You will like some of the tools; you will find others harder to work with. In the long-term this is probably the most important criterion for putting together a program for a creative session. The experience of the group also plays a role here. If the group consists of inexperienced participants, the simpler methods will be more suitable. If the group is more experienced, you can work with slightly less common methods (as long as the session leader is well acquainted with them!). You can even experiment a bit.

The tool selector should be used as an aid for compiling a program, but it can also be used to determine a reading order when reading this book. Let yourself be guided by interesting titles of tools you come across in the selector, and decide on your own preferences.

Tool selector

	Tool Stage	1	2	3	4	5	6	7	8	9	10	pag.
1	5xW and H	X		X	X						X	33
2	appreciation	X		X								35
3	mind map	X		X	X		X	X		X	X	37
4	concept map	X		X	X		X	X		X	X	39
5	reformulation			X								41
6	goal orientation			X								43
7	low hanging fruits			X	X					X		45
8	SWOT analysis			X	X					X		48
9	nominal group technique			X	X					X		50
10	process decision program chart (PDPC)			X	X					X		52
11	cause and effect diagram			X	X							54
12	flow-chart			X	X					X	X	56
13	process map			X	X					X	X	58
14	checklist			X	X					X		60
15	chain association						X	X				62
16	flower association						X	X				64
17	classical brainstorming						X	X				66
18	brainwriting 6.3.5.						X	X				68
19	dynamic brainwriting						X	X				70
20	ping-pong brainstorming						X	X				72
21	brainlining						X	X				74
22	oracle method						X	X				76
23	wishful thinking						X	X				78
24	alternatives						X	X				80
25	presuppositions						X	X				82
26	the criminal circle						X	X				84
27	changing the point of entry						X	X				86
28	natural analogy						X	X				88

	Tool	Stage	1	2	3	4	5	6	7	8	9	10	pag.
29	personal analogy							X	X				90
30	fantasy analogy							X	X				92
31	metaphors							X	X				95
32	random information							X	X				97
33	morphological box							X	X				99
34	matec							X	X				101
35	visual stimulation							X	X				103
36	poetic stimulation							X	X				105
37	provocative sub-division							X	X				108
38	provocative questioning							X	X				110
39	design method							X	X				112
40	clustering										X	X	114
41	list of criteria										X		116
42	hits										X		118
43	WRA method										X		120
44	resistance table										X		122
45	influence analysis										X		124
46	PMI										X		126
47	NAA method										X		128
48	elimination race										X		130
49	solution resistance table										X	X	131
50	devil/angel's advocate										X	X	133
51	action plan											X	135

1. 5XW AND H

Flow position:	1, 3, 4 and 10
Participants:	1 - 20
Requisites:	pen, paper, marker pen, flip chart, 🖥

It is a good idea to use a standard list of questions during the problem formulation and analysis phases and when drawing up a plan of action.

Method

Answer the following questions:

Who?	Who is involved, who has to implement it?
What?	What is the problem, what has to happen?
Where?	In what situation is it happening, where must the solution be implemented?
When?	How long has the problem already existed, when does it have to be solved by?
Why?	What is the (actual) objective?
How?	How were solutions that have already been tried out formulated, and how does the new solution have to be introduced?

Assignment

For the last ten years, you have gone jogging with the same group of people three times a week. You now have to organize a party. Work out the details using the questions listed above.

Tips and tricks

- Use a standard mind map (see tool 3) with Who, What, etc.
- Also ask the provocative questions "what if?" and "how else?"

Flow position: 1 and 3
Participants: 2 - 4
Requisites: pen, paper, marker pens, flip chart

Appreciation is a simple, effective analysis technique which gets the maximum possible amount of information out of a simple fact. By repeatedly asking a simple question, you rapidly get to the underlying problem and the measures to be taken.

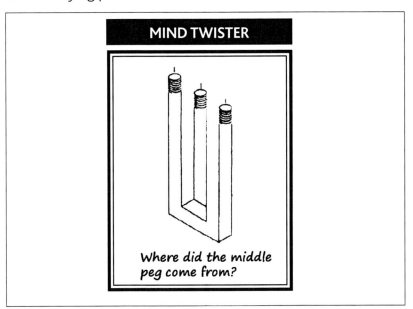

MIND TWISTER

Where did the middle peg come from?

Method
Starting with the simple fact, ask the question "so?". In other words, what are the consequences of that fact? Keep asking until all the possible consequences have been considered

Example
An example taken from the residential or utility construction industry:

36 Fact: it poured with rain last night.

So?

The ground is damp.

So?

It'll soon turn into a mud bath.

So?

When lots of trucks drive over the same piece of ground, we'll eventually have problems.

So?

Use a metal underlay if possible or be prepared for delay.

Flow position:	1, 3, 4, 6, 7, 9 and 10
Participants:	1 - 20
Requisites:	pen, paper, colored pencils, marker pens, flip chart, 💻

Developed by Tony Buzan, mind maps are an effective method of noting down and generating ideas by means of association. You can use mind maps for making notes (in lectures, meetings and for preparing presentations) and for making summaries, for studying, taking minutes of meetings, for individual or collective brainstorming sessions, planning, designing training courses and analyzing situations.

Method
- Only use key words, drawings etc.
- Note down the subject in the middle of a blank piece of paper, for example in a circle or a cloud.
- Think from the point of view of "Who, What, Where, When, Why and How".
- Draw lines from the middle for the sub-themes.
- Use colors.
- When making an individual mind map, use blank paper, preferably A3 landscape format

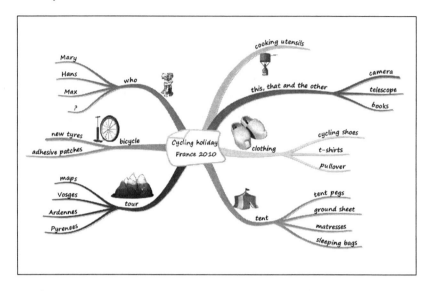

Assignment

Make a mind map containing your activities for the rest of the day.

Flow position:	1, 3, 4, 6, 7, 9 and 10
Participants:	1 - 20
Requisites:	pen, paper, colored pencils, marker pens, flip chart, 🖥

Concept mapping is a technique for graphically reproducing concepts and their mutual relationships. Concept maps can be used to collect known information, generate ideas and visualize complex relationships. While mind maps only contain one central concept, concept maps contain several.

A mind map can be reproduced as a branch; a concept map is a network.

Concept maps consist of nodes and labeled connecting lines.

Method

1. Note down the most important concepts (possibly on Post-it® notes).

2. Arrange these so that topics that are related can be placed next to each other (keep the concepts that are not relevant at the moment separate).

3. Draw lines/arrows between the concepts that you think are related.

4. Note the type of relationship on the lines or arrows.

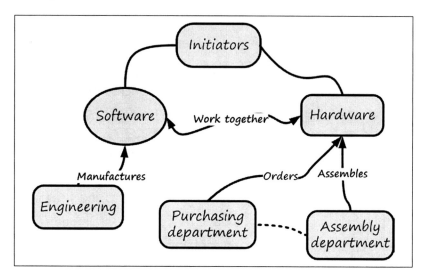

The example is a simple one. However, concept maps can be very complex and require a lot of attention.

Assignment

Make a concept map containing the following concepts; photographic equipment, photographs, bicycle, fossils and factory.

Tips and tricks

Try combining several techniques e.g. concept mapping and mind mapping.

Flow position:	3
Participants:	1 - 20
Requisites:	pen, paper, marker pen, flip chart, 🖳

What is the real problem? To avoid starting with a problem that is incorrect or inadequately formulated it is a good idea to reformulate it in various ways. The aim is to get a complete and correct view of the subject matter and to arrive at a formulation that best describes the problem. In doing so you also extend the involvement of the participants. If it appears that the problem actually consists of several sub-problems, deal with them separately. Start with one single concrete target.

Method

Try to find as many reformulations as possible (15 to 20) and then make a choice (collectively). You could generate a definitive reformulation from the crucial data in the various reformulations you have come up with.

1. Summarize the problem in a short question that begins with:

"How can I ... "
"How can Mabel ... "
"How can we ... "

2. Follow this with:

" ... ensure that ... "
" ... achieve ... "
" ... do ... "

3. Check whether the reformulation describes the essence of the problem.

Assignment

Pick a problem have you been thinking about for some time now. Think of at least 10 reformulations for this problem.

Tips and tricks

- Take the core concepts from the problem definition as the point of departure.
- Get several participants to each make a number of reformulations for themselves. This increases involvement.
- Pick the "furthest removed" reformulation.
- Make use of the "Wishful Thinking" technique (see tool 23) as well.

6. GOAL ORIENTATION

Flow position: 3
Participants: 1 - 20
Requisites: pen, paper, marker pen, flip chart

Is the actual goal clear? During the reformulation phase it is important to determine what the actual goal is. Is the problem your car that is due for replacement or is it the accessibility of the company where you work?

Method

1. Describe the actual goal.

2. If this goal does not agree with the problem originally formulated, reformulate it.

3. Determine the new criteria which the solutions must meet.

Example

A company establishes that its quality system is unsatisfactory. The quality manual is seen as being the problem because it is insufficiently up-to-date. The quality department is instructed to write a new quality manual. Upon inquiry it appears that the problem actually lies with the employees and the management, who do not want to spend time on a critical evaluation of the day-to-day processes.

44   Assignment

During the course of one week note down each problem with which you are confronted and ask yourself what the actual goal is or what it should be.

Tips and tricks

- Ask yourself what the actual goal is for each problem.
- Ask "why?" at least 5 times.

7. LOW HANGING FRUITS

Flow position:	3, 4 and 9
Participants:	1 - 20
Requisites:	pen, paper, marker pen, flip chart, adhesive dots (red, green, black and yellow)

When choosing between various items such as problems and/or possible solutions it is a good idea to determine which are the easiest cherries to pick. By making a personal evaluation you can determine which of the items yield a lot with little effort. In doing so you will also be able to indicate the extent of your own influence. This evaluation is reproduced in graphic form.

Method

1. Write down the various items (problems, ideas) from which a choice has to be made, on a flip chart.
2. Number the items.
3. Give each team member half as many adhesive dots as there are items;
   red to indicate the effort that will probably be necessary,
   green to indicate the expected yield,
   black to indicate your own influence on the solution of the problem or the realization of the idea.
   Example: for 17 items you will have eight red dots to measure the effort, eight green dots to measure the result and eight black dots to indicate the extent of your own influence.
4. Everyone evaluates the items from their own point of view.
5. Stick on the various dots in accordance with the effort you require to solve the problem, the expected result or yield and

the expected extent of your own influence.

6. In order to give some items extra weight you can, for instance, use a maximum of two dots of one color, for example, one red dot for the effort, two green dots for the yield and two black dots for your own influence.

7. When everyone is finished you can count the dots.

8. After you have evaluated the dots you can reproduce the effort and the yield in graphic form:

   note the numbers of the items on yellow dots,

   then place these on the problem overview according to the evaluation of effort and yield,

   then note the value for your own influence on each dot.

9. In the graphic below you will find the items for which the yield is greater than the effort at the bottom-right of the triangle; the effort is relatively higher than the yield at the top-left of the triangle.

10. You will find the interesting items at the bottom-right of the triangle.

Example

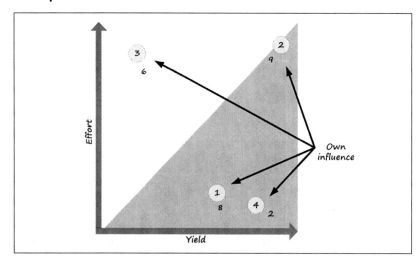

According to the graphic, the item with number 1 has a high
yield with relatively little effort and a high level of own influence
(8). The item with number 4 yields even more with less effort,
however, the level of own influence is clearly less (2). For
example, if a choice has to be made from several problems that
need solving, the problem with number 1 seems to be the most
obvious "cherry" to be picked.

8. SWOT ANALYSIS

Flow position: 3, 4 and 9
Participants: 1 - 20
Requisites: pen, paper, marker pen, flip chart, 🖥

SWOT stands for Strengths, Weaknesses, Opportunities and Threats and is an effective method of identifying strengths and weaknesses and examining opportunities and threats. The results can often be enlightening both in that they can indicate what needs to be done as well as enabling you to see problems in their correct perspective.

Method
Draw a table and note down in it the answers to the questions:

- **Strengths:** what are the plus points and benefits
- **Weaknesses:** what is going wrong and what can be improved
- **Opportunities:** where do the opportunities lie, are there any interesting trends (new technology, changed markets, government policies, population profiles, lifestyles, local, regional, national events)
- **Threats:** what obstacles do you see (what are your competitors doing, have the requirements for the job changed, product or service, is changed technology a threat to your position, is your financial situation under threat?).

Example   49

Strengths	Weaknesses
e.g. •Simple to use •Cheap •...	e.g. •Awareness •Limited application •...
Opportunities	Threats
e.g. •No competitors yet •...	e.g. •Easy to copy •...

Assignment

You are wondering whether a product or service that you supply (to an internal or external customer) is still satisfactory. Do a SWOT analysis on how you view this product or service.

Tips and tricks

Answer the questions from your own point of view and from the point of view of those you deal with (internal or external customers, competitors). Be realistic and honest.

9. NOMINAL GROUP TECHNIQUE

Flow position:	3, 4 and 9
Participants:	4 - 20
Requisites:	pen, paper, marker pen, flip chart, Post-it notes®

The nominal group technique is used to gather problems and possible causes of and/or solutions to the problems concerning a specific theme and to reach consensus with a group quickly.

Method
1. Ask all participants to name or write down the problem, the cause of the problem, the solution or, in general terms, the theme that they find the most important.
2. Generate a list of these items (remove duplications and ask for explanations on unclear points) and mark these with a letter.
3. Each participant individually ranks the items.
4. Collect the results and count them up per item. The item with the highest score is the most important to the group.
5. Discuss the results.

Example   51

item	Mabel	Horace	Bryan	Edgar	Anne	total
A	4	5	2	2	1	14
B	5	4	5	3	5	22
C	3	1	3	4	4	15
D	1	2	1	5	2	11
E	2	3	4	1	3	13

A group of five people have to choose one of the possible solutions A, B, C, D, or E. They evaluate the solutions individually (e.g. with Post-it® notes) with a scale of between 1 and 5.

Solution B scores highest and will be worked on first.

Assignment

Apply the nominal group technique at the next meeting at which a choice has to be made which would otherwise result in lengthy discussions.

Tips and tricks

- The "low hanging fruits" technique (tool 7) can also be used in the situation outlined above.
- Use a scale of 1 to 4 for fewer than 20 items, use a scale of 1 to 6 for 20-35 items and use a scale of 1 to 8 for more than 35 items.

10. PROCESS DECISION PROGRAM CHART (PDPC)

Flow position:	3, 4 and 9
Participants:	1 - 20
Requisites:	pen, paper, marker pen, flip chart, 💻

You can use the PDPC technique to map out the possible alternatives in problem situations and for the implementation of a plan.

Method

1. Determine the steps to be taken and place these in the correct order
2. Make a tree diagram, horizontal or vertical
3. Identify the possible risks for each step
4. Determine possible solutions and/or explanations for each of these problems and note these down.

Example

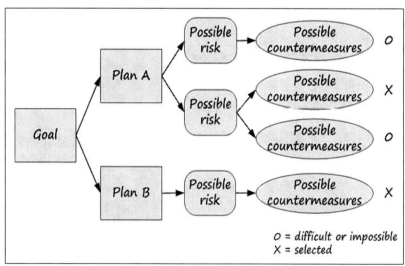

Assignment

Your bathroom needs renovating. But you need to ensure that you can keep on using it while the work is going on. Work out two possible plans. Then make a process decision program chart (PDPC), evaluate the possible risks and think of possible countermeasures.

Tips and tricks

- PDPC elements can be easily added to a flow-chart (tool 12) or a process map (tool 13).
- Instead of determining the risks we can turn it around and determine the opportunities.
- Use brainstorming (tools 17-21) and the nominal group technique (tool 9) to identify the risks.

11. CAUSE AND EFFECT DIAGRAM

Flow position: 3 and 4
Participants: 1 - 20
Requisites: pen, paper, marker pen, flip chart, 🖳

A cause and effect diagram (also known as a herringbone diagram or an Ishikawa diagram) is an analysis instrument that is used to map out the possible causes of a problem in a structured manner.

Method
1. Agree a word or term with a view to highlighting the problem briefly and clearly.
2. Brainstorm on the possible causes of the problem.
3. Divide the causes into a number of categories, if possible the following: "man", "method", "material" and "resources".

Draw up the cause and effect analysis:
- Put the indication of the problem in the "problem" box at the head of the herringbone diagram.
- Put the categories (man, method, material and resources) of the causes in the boxes at the beginning of the sideways arrows.
- Put the causes per category that you have come up with in the brainstorming session in the diagram by drawing horizontal arrows towards the sideways arrows. This creates the herringbone pattern. Subordinate causes can then be indicated by drawing more slanting arrows on the horizontal arrows (not shown in the example).
- Determine the most detailed level of each cause by keeping on asking the question "Why does this happen?". Repeat

the question at least five times until you have an answer.
The ultimate main cause must be so specific that you end
up with a measurable verdict.

Choose a small number of causes (3 to 5) at the highest level
which probably have the greatest impact on the problem.

Example

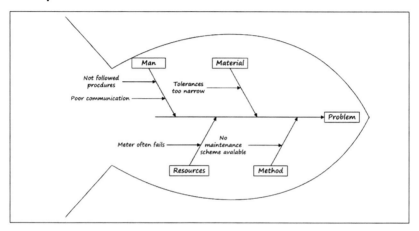

Assignment
Using a cause and effect diagram, determine why the telephone
is not answered quickly enough.

Tips and tricks
- Make "mini" cause and effect diagrams with a flow-chart
  (see tool 12) or an influence analysis (see tool 45).
- Make use of the "low hanging fruits" technique (tool 7) to
  determine which causes should be actioned first.

12. FLOW-CHART

Flow position:	3, 4, 9 and 10
Participants:	1 - 20
Requisites:	pen, paper, marker pen, flip chart, 🖳

A flow-chart clearly sets out the stages in a process by means of symbols. It is used to define and analyze processes. A flow-chart of the actual situation thus forms a basis for standardization and action for improvement. Once solutions have been found for any problems there may be, a flow-chart of the required situation can be made.

Method
1. Determine the limits of the process; what is the starting point and what is the end point.
2. Establish the stages within the process.
   Brainstorm on all the activities that fall within the process limits you have defined. Think about the order of the activities and what decisions have to be taken.
3. Draw the flow-chart. The following symbols are the most common:

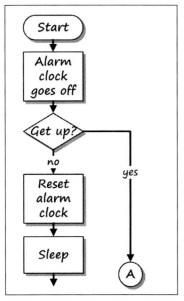

An oval indicates the beginning and end of the process.

A rectangle indicates an activity; there is usually just one arrow entering the box and one arrow coming out of it.

A diamond indicates the point where a decision has to be taken.

A circle with a letter or number identifies a transition to another page.

Arrows show the direction of the flow of the process.

4. Analyze the flow-chart. Note things like:

• the duration of activities and decisions
• repetitions of actions (rework)
• activities without value added
• activities that are regularly disrupted.

Assignment

Complete the sample flow-chart as if you had decided to get up after all. The process ends when you shut your front door behind you.

Tips and tricks

It is often difficult to decide how much detail a flow-chart should go into. Past experience and commonsense are the most important guidelines.

58   13. PROCESS MAP

Flow position:	3, 4, 9 and 10
Participants:	1 - 20
Requisites:	pen, paper, marker pen, flip chart, large sheets of paper, 💻

A process map is a variation on the flow-chart. In addition to the flow of the process, a process map also indicates what functions are significant within the process. It therefore also highlights the organizational context.

Method
1. Determine the limits of the process; what is the starting point and what is the end point.
2. Establish the stages within the process.
   Brainstorm on all the activities that fall within the process limits you have defined. Think about the order of the activities and what decisions have to be taken.
3. Establish who is/are involved.
4. Draw the process flow from left to right, using the symbols as used in a flow-chart.

Example

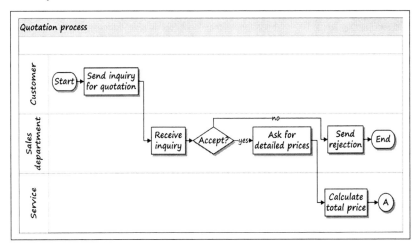

Assignment

Draw up a process map for preparations for a vacation in which several people/functions play a role (e.g. traveling companions, travel agent, garage etc.).

Tips and tricks

- Make your first draft using Post-it® notes (this enables rapid adaptation).
- Limit your first draft to no more than 12-20 process stages.
- Using color provides a third dimension; e.g. use to distinguish between activities that actually have value added and those which only cost money.

14. CHECKLIST

Flow position: 3, 4 and 9
Participants: 1 - 20
Requisites: pen, paper, marker pen, flip chart, 🖳

A checklist is used to establish up front any requirements and wishes which will be relevant to the solutions.

Method

After the phase in which the problem is formulated with the problem owner:

1. Make a note of the requirements and wishes.
2. Give all the requirements and wishes a weighting factor (e.g. using a scale of 1-10 or 1-3).
3. During the elaboration phase, use the checklist to evaluate the solutions you have come up with (see list of criteria).

Example

You are looking out for a new bicycle. A checklist with wishes and requirements might read as follows: (weighting factors 1-3 in column 3)

✓	63 cm frame	3
✓	for use around town	1
	suitable for leisure use	3
	suitable for use on vacation	3
✓	racing handlebars	2
	color: black	1
	meets legal requirements	1
	double lock	3
	unattractive to thieves	2

Assignment

Go to bicycle shops and gather information on standard and customized bicycles. Choose three bicycles which appeal to you. Using the above checklist, draw up a list of criteria and decide whether the bicycles you have selected adequately meet the requirements and wishes you have formulated.

Tips and tricks

- It is useful to draw up the final checklist in order of importance, starting with the most important (weighting factor).
- Be aware that a checklist is subjective.
- With a checklist you build on existing models; it will probably exclude any really innovative solutions (what do you think of a reclining bicycle in the above example?).

15. CHAIN ASSOCIATION

Flow position:	6 and 7
Number of participants:	1 - 20
Requisites:	pen, paper

The chain association is a tool intended to enable you to (temporarily) distance yourself from a problem and to return to the problem with a force to fit. By jumping from word to word (association), from thought to thought, with a good chance of reaching turning points, it is very likely that you will come across new points of view which may lead to other (better?) solutions.

Method
1. Pick a starting word relating to the problem definition.
2. Make a number of association chains.
3. Choose from them a word which is far removed from the problem.
4. Generate new ideas from the word by means of association.

Example

turning point

fruit peel – apple – tree – root – calculation – math – school - youth

Assignment
- Get from Amsterdam to Paris in seven words using chain association.
- Make three different chain associations of five words, starting with Buck.

The chain association can be created using just a starting word or an end word, but can also be done with a starting word as well as an end word (guided chain).

MIND TWISTER

Drawing exercise

The aim of this little game is to lower the 'drawing threshold' of the participants. Ask one of the participants to illustrate a specific concept to the group by doing a drawing of it on a flip-chart. No word may be used at all. The person who guesses the word becomes the next 'victim'.

Than What?

16. FLOWER ASSOCIATION

Flow position:	6 and 7
Participants:	1 - 20
Requisites:	pen, paper, marker pen, flip chart

The flower association is a basic technique with which the environment of a problem can be explored by means of thoughts running in different directions. All aspects surrounding a core word from the problem definition can be noted by means of free association, even thoughts which at first glance have nothing to do with the matter in hand. The new insights that this method can yield are of great importance in finding creative solutions.

Method
1. Choose a starting word, usually a core word from the problem definition.
2. Make a number of flower associations.
3. From the results, pick a word which seems to be far removed from the problem definition.
4. Try to develop new ideas from this word and note them down.

Example

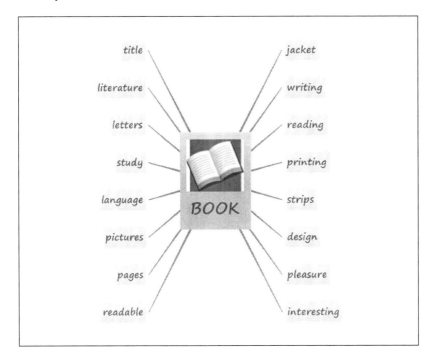

Assignment
- Make a flower association around the word "advisor".
- Make a flower association with at least 10 derivatives,
  including a number of non-clichéd associations
  surrounding the word "flower".

Tips and tricks
To obtain good results from a flower association, you have to
keep at it: once your ideas have been exhausted (so that you end
up with a predominance of clichéd associations), you will have
to force yourself to continue and to add just a few more words.
You should then be aiming for non-clichéd associations. You
should also ensure that no chain associations occur. Give it a try.

17. CLASSIC BRAINSTORMING

Flow position:	6 and 7
Participants:	4 - 20
Requisites:	pen, paper, marker pen, flip chart

The classic brainstorming session, developed by Alex Osborn, is a creative group process in which the emphasis is on "cross-pollination" by each other's utterances. The ideas put forward by the various participants are used by the others as the basis for associations. The ideas will then keep coming. This method is often used as the starting point for other techniques.

Method

1. Make sure that the problem is set out in clear, concise terms.
2. Have all participants put forward ideas.
3a. Mention now and again that the participants can take their inspiration from other people's ideas.
3b. Every now and again, pick one of the ideas as a new source of inspiration and carry on from there.

Assignment

1. In a small group, try generating as many ideas as possible (i.e. as fast as possible!) with the aid of a simple problem definition.
2. With the same group and the same problem definition, try out step 3b of the method.

Tips and tricks

- Brainstorming and "purging" (see chapter 4, "Frame for a Creative Process") are very close to each other; there is hardly any difference between them. However, by placing slightly more emphasis on association, you can in fact achieve just that little bit more.

- Because this method is so simple, it is also suitable for use as a warm-up or intermezzo. Try it out with a jolly, light-hearted or even ridiculous problem definition to bring humor into it. Something really crazy in between is a good way of relaxing. You are then "charged up" again and ready to continue.

18. BRAINWRITING 6.3.5.

Flow position: 6 and 7
Participants: 3 - 10
Requisites: pen, paper, marker pen, flip chart

This written variation of the classic brainstorming session takes its name from the following method: 6 participants write down 3 new ideas in 5 minutes. These rules do not actually have to be applied so strictly; one or two participants more or less is fine, as is slightly more or less time. The problem definition is also important here.

Method
1. Hand out the brainwriting forms and describe the problem with background information.
2. The participants then reformulate the problem in their own words on the top of the form.
3. Everyone then writes down their first three ideas on the form.
4. After five minutes (or when the group is ready) the forms are all moved round to the next person.
5. The participants read the ideas written down, take their inspiration from them and write three new ideas below them.
6. Repeat steps 4 and 5 until the form is full.

Assignment
Use this method in a group of six people, e.g. colleagues, for a minor problem that really needs to be dealt with.

Example   69

Brainwriting 6.3.5		
reformulation		
Idea 1	Idea 2	Idea 3

Tips and tricks

- Try using this method with a group of people you know, some of whom never open their mouths and some who have theirs open all the time. The advantage of this method is that everybody has to have an equal say.
- To simplify the grouping of the ideas, it is a good idea to use Post-it® notes that fit into the squares in the form. This saves a lot of re-writing.

19. DYNAMIC BRAINWRITING

Flow position:	6 and 7
Participants:	1 - 20
Requisites:	pen, paper, marker pen, flip chart, Post-it® notes

This method is derived from the classic brainstorming method. The dynamism is achieved by noting ideas on loose adhesive stickers and by adding random information if you think that the flow of ideas is about to stagnate or needs a new stimulus. An additional advantage is that the adhesive stickers are easy to move about and can easily be clustered at the end of the session so as to form the start of the critical phase.

Method
1. Based on the collective reformulation of the problem, write down the first ideas on adhesive stickers and stick these on the table.
2. Everyone then moves up a place.
3. Note down your new ideas based on what you have in front of you on the table.
4. After a few of these rounds, additional stimulus can be given by putting forward random information (a random word or subject).
5. When you decide to stop, all write down your final ideas.
6. Every participant then makes an initial clustering of the ideas on the table in front of him or her.

Read "Random Information" (tool 32) to support point 4 of the above method.

Tips and tricks

- Make sure this method is actually dynamic. Do not place chairs around the table; have the participants stand and walk around.
- Make sure the table is empty apart from the problem definition and the Post-it® notes. No distractions.
- When you change places, participants can move to any other place if this is agreed beforehand.
- Take advantage of the fact that the Post-it® notes are adhesive. For instance, you could also use a suitable method such as clustering, during the critical phase.

20. PING-PONG BRAINSTORMING

Flow position:	6 and 7
Participants:	2
Requisites:	pen, paper, marker pen, flip chart

This method of brainstorming is intended to bring about a structured brainstorming session during a discussion between two people. Normally this method is not often used in a discussion between (just) two people. However, because it is so simple in structure, it is possible to achieve good results with a team this small.

Method
1. Formulate the problem clearly together and decide who will do the writing.
2. Take it in turns to put forward ideas or potential solutions (taking between 10 and 15 seconds each).
3. In particular, try to build on the other person's ideas; if necessary, only put forward associations.
4. After five minutes, check whether the flow of ideas still relates sufficiently to the problem in hand.
5. Start again from step 2, if necessary from a different point of view.

Assignment
Try this method the next time you talk to ... (a friend, a colleague, your neighbor) about a problem.

Tips and tricks

- Have the other person do the writing after 5 minutes.
- If you think that the ideas will come thick and fast, you can decide to resume the ping-pong discussion and continue working on it later.
- Practice has shown that this method is not always easy to use with any random pairing of people. Experience will show who the best partners are.

MIND TWISTER

Paperclip

Give each person a paperclip and then ask them the following question:

"Besides using it as a paperclip, what other uses can you think of for this little bit of iron wire?"

21. BRAINLINING

Flow position: 6 and 7
Participants: 1 - 20
Requisites: computer network

This brainstorming technique is specifically intended for use on the Internet or intranet or other computer networks. The method is similar to the usual brainstorming session, but additionally makes use of modern technology, which has a number of advantages. The biggest advantage is in some situations that you do not actually have to be physically in the same place.

Method
1. As the facilitator, ensure that all participants are acquainted with the use and the capabilities of the computer and the software.
2. Organize the session so that everybody is ready at their computer at the same time, and ensure that the participants all have a clear definition of the problem at their own location.
3. The participants can then type in their own ideas. Depending on the system, all the participants will be able to read the ideas directly or they will be made visible to everybody by the facilitator.
4. The participants can keep typing in their own ideas and potential solutions, inspired by other people's ideas.
5. Depending on the situation, the problem definition, the group and the number of ideas, the facilitator can intervene and add

new information in order to increase the number of ideas and
to extend the variation in the ideas.

Assignment

Find out within your own organization whether this method is possible, and if so, how to approach it.

Tips and tricks

- You can of course take a lot longer over the session, with each participant working on the flow of ideas in his own time. (Not actually a session; participants will not be working on the problem simultaneously, but the method can still yield results.)
- This method can also be used to work with participants who do not know each other and in fact do not get to know each other. An anonymous brainstorming session is also possible. This may in some cases open up new horizons and break down barriers for the participants.

22. THE ORACLE METHOD

Flow position:	6 and 7
Participants:	4 - 10
Requisites:	Internet, Intranet, mail, E-mail, fax, etc

In this method, the participants are not physically in the same place; they do not even need to know each other. The session leader forms the central point for the flow of information. It is advisable to use this method only for very general problems. The session leader must have a certain amount of experience with creativity because he or she has to act as the oracle for incoming information without adding value judgments.

Method

1. The participants are informed of the method and the problem definition and are provided with background information if necessary.
2. The participants send their first ideas to the session leader (no more than three). This is done independently of one another.
3. All ideas are combined by the session leader to form one (complex) idea, the oracle.
4. The oracle is sent to the participants and they then use it as inspiration for new ideas or comments.
5. Steps 3 and 4 are repeated until the session leader is able to present a number of concrete ideas and potential solutions.
6. If necessary, a complete report of the process can be sent to the participants.

Example 77

Problem: "What ideas can we come up with to add to the agenda for a company party?".

Ideas: 1. Bowling competition

2. Boat trip

3. Dinner/dance

4. Cabaret

5. Slide show

Oracle no. 1: Organize a boat trip with a slide show about a bowling competition, with a cabaret dinner at the same time

Assignment

In a random session or series of ideas, try to arrive at a formulation containing a combination of various ideas; the oracle.

Tips and tricks

- Because the participants in this method do not actually have to meet, you can take your time and complete each phase in small steps.
- It is difficult for the session leader not to make value judgments on the various ideas when he or she is making the oracle. This can be avoided by combining the ideas to form the oracle together with someone else.

23. WISHFUL THINKING

Flow position:	6 and 7
Participants:	1 - 20
Requisites:	pen, paper, marker pen, flip chart

Which solution would be your preferred one? Wishful thinking is a technique based on the ideal solution. You then try to achieve this.

Method
After formulating or reformulating the problem, go through the following steps:

1. Think of possible ideal solutions (without restricting yourself in any way) and note these down.
2. Pick two or three ideal solutions.
3. Go through them one at a time and think of ideas which would enable you to achieve your ideal solution.

Example/assignment
You see that the various television stations have a number of excellent programs in their packages. However, the commercial breaks thoroughly spoil your enjoyment. One of the ideas is to start your own television station for yourself and a large group of friends and acquaintances. Think of a second "ideal solution" and then generate ideas as to how you can achieve these solutions.

MIND TWISTER

Malapropisms

These are 'incorrect' expressions in which two sayings, adages or expressions are confused:

• 'Half a loaf is better than two in the bush'
• 'An early bird catches no moss.'
• 'Splitting hairs on a bald man's head.'

Try to find expressions which you can 'reconstruct' so as to make good examples of malapropisms.

24. ALTERNATIVES

Flow position:	6 and 7
Participants:	1 - 20
Requisites:	pen, paper, marker pen, flip chart

Looking for alternatives is a basic technique which can be implemented independently, but is also often used as part of other methods. Keeping on looking for alternatives, even past the point where you become frustrated because nothing seems to be coming, is a way of breaking through thought patterns and arriving at new potential solutions.

Method
1. Try and find as many normal alternative solutions to the problem as possible.
2. Once the flow has dried up, try to think of another 2 or 3 alternatives.
3. Throw open all the floodgates of thought by applying the rules of creative thinking (see chapter 3).
4. All alternatives, whether possible or impossible, must be put forward. Use your powers of association and imagination.
5. Here too, pressure can again be exacted to come up with another 3 alternatives once the flow of ideas seems to be drying up.

Example

Divide a square into four pieces equal in shape and area. (Use the two empty squares for practicing).

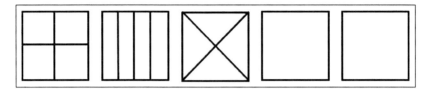

Assignment

Let yourself go completely to find possible and impossible alternatives to the problem:

How will I celebrate my 20th, 30th, 40th, 50th birthday?

Tips and tricks

To highlight where the so-called frustration point lies (this differs from person to person) and how that feels, a simple exercise can be useful:

Draw 10 empty squares on a piece of paper and try to divide each of the squares into four parts equal in shape and area. Once you have filled the first sheet, make another one, just until you start to feel frustrated. Then carry on!

25. PRESUPPOSITIONS

Flow position:	6 and 7
Participants:	1 - 20
Requisites:	pen, paper, marker pen, flip chart

With presuppositions you make use of the fact that with crucial concepts (in a problem definition) you always start consciously or unconsciously with a number of assumptions. By now tracking down these assumptions and by seeking to temporarily eliminate solutions or replace them with alternatives, new insights and potential solutions can be given a chance. In doing so, this method lowers our thought threshold and makes it possible to pursue other thought patterns.

Method
1. Look for a crucial term in the problem definition.
2. Determine which assumptions pertain to this term and note these down.
3. Look for an alternative for this presupposition or eliminate it completely.
4. Generate ideas that suddenly appear possible as a result.
5. Repeat the whole phase with other crucial terms or with other alternatives until you have enough ideas.

Example
"What is the best way to automate this department?". This problem, which is often heard in business, presupposes a number of things. One of these presuppositions is that the relevant department would function better if it were automated. By replacing the term "automate" with another (e.g. "optimize",

"improve", "make it more productive"), whole new angles are opened up and alternative ideas can be put on the table.

Assignment

In the problem below, try to determine a number of crucial terms and indicate a number of presuppositions:

"How do I tell my boss that I want to have tomorrow off?"

Then think of a number of alternatives for these presuppositions and look for new potential solutions which then present themselves.

Tips and tricks

There is another method that can be used to discover the presuppositions surrounding a problem. Try to note the collective characteristics from the first series of ideas. These often point to presuppositions. Note these down and continue with step 3 of the method.

84   26. THE CRIMINAL CIRCLE

Flow position: 6 - 7
Participants: 1 - 20
Requisites: pen, paper, marker pen, flip chart

The criminal circle refers to
the secret wish that people
have to do things that they
are not allowed to do. The effort
that this thought alone frees up
provides enormous creativity.

Method
1. Make sure that the problem is clearly reformulated.
2. Give the participants the assignment to think of solutions
   with a criminal slant, solutions which are not allowed.
3. Note down these ideas and use them as a source of
   inspiration for "legal ideas".
4. Begin again at step 2 when the flow of ideas stops. Now
   give them a specific area of crime (such as smuggling, fraud,
   deception, liquidation etc.).

Assignment
Think of criminal solutions for the following problem:

"Will we be able to develop two new products in six months?"

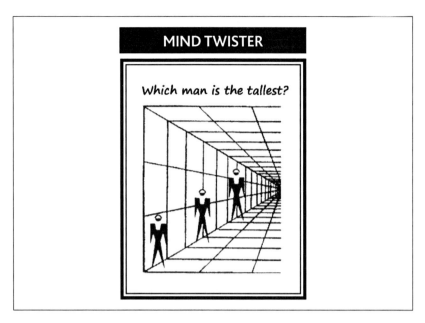

Tips and tricks

- Newspapers are full of criminal cases every day. Use these as a source of inspiration.
- Try converting criminal ideas into legal ideas.

27. CHANGING THE POINT OF ENTRY

Flow position: 6 and 7
Participants: 1 - 20
Requisites: pen, paper, marker pen, flip chart

By adapting the problem definition in a provocative manner, the point of entry, or the aspect from which the problem is approached, can be changed. This can be done in different ways, such as by replacing one of the terms in the problem definition by another one, or by changing the order of the various terms. The reformulation of the problem definition that comes about in this way offers ways of looking at the problem from a different point of view and coming up with new solutions and alternatives.

Method
1. Make sure the problem definition is clear and concise;
2a. Replace one of the terms in the problem definition by an alternative;
2b. Change the order of the terms in the problem definition around (the subject becomes the direct object, etc.);
3. Try to come up with new potential solutions and ideas on the basis of this reformulation;
4. Repeat 2a or 2b to obtain even more potential solutions.

Example
Everyone knows the classic turnaround from the newspaper, "dog bites man - man bites dog". To indicate how different the reformulations can be, there follow two examples of the following problem:

- How do I get gas out of my tank at night with no money?
- How does my neighbor get gas in my tank at night with no money?

So there are a large number of alternative problem definitions you could come up with which enable you to look at things from a completely new angle.

Assignment

- Make two different reformulations with different points of entry for the problem: "How can I keep my office tidy?".
- Look at the new angles that this provides.

Tips and tricks

Not every problem definition lends itself this easily to a large number of different points of entry. In that case, pick one which would seem to fit and use that one. Always make sure that the problem has been formulated clearly and with one objective in mind.

28. NATURAL ANALOGY

Flow position:	6 and 7
Participants:	1 - 20
Requisites:	pen, paper, marker pen, flip chart

The natural analogy method is a floating technique which uses more or less random associations. By comparing completely different concepts with one another, you can distance yourself from the problem. The similarities that can nonetheless be found between the concepts or the forced associations between the random concept and the problem definition can provide new aspects and angles which may contribute towards finding a creative solution to the problem.

Method
1. Pick out the most characteristic concept from the problem definition.
2. Pick a random word or concept that has nothing to do with the term from the problem definition.
3. Try to find as many similarities between these two concepts as possible; in doing so, do not stop at the first series of logical solutions, but keep going, if necessary with far-fetched similarities.
4. Try to find new solutions and ideas from this list of similarities.

Example

Problem definition:	"Think up new products or services for a company that applies coatings to metal objects."
Characteristic concept:	'coating'
Random term:	'bottle'
Similarities:	smooth outer surface, finished product, color, label, thermal process, clean etc.
Possible ideas:	enameling of products, cleaning coated surfaces -> recoating.

Assignment

Find as many similarities as possible between the following concepts:

- pen and bed,
- spoon and cook.

Tips and tricks

- Make sure the concepts used in this method can be visualized or drawn. This creates more opportunities to find similarities and to visualize them.
- Instead of looking for similarities between the two concepts (step 3), you can also look for specific characteristics in the random term. In step 4 you can then look for new ideas inspired by this list of characteristics.

Both methods can also be used very well alongside one another.

29. PERSONAL ANALOGY

Flow position: 6 and 7
Participants: 1 - 20
Requisites: pen, paper, marker pen, flip chart

The use of the personal analogy method is definitely not simple, but can produce excellent results when properly used. Changing the subject (or one of the other elements) of the problem definition into "I" demands an enormous degree of empathy in order to arrive at practical but creative new ideas.

Method
1. Decide which subject (or thing) is the most essential for the problem definition.
2. Replace this word by "I" and make a note of the new formulation.
3. Try to come up with new angles and ideas by demanding the maximum possible amount of empathy.
4. Link this back to the original problem definition.

Assignment
Start with the following problem formulation and replace one of the nouns by 'I' or 'me':

"How can company X make its products easier for customers to recognize on the shelves?".

Try out a number of different possibilities and make a note of the new angles and ideas that this brings about.

Tips and tricks

- You can generate a large number of ideas in a short time by distributing the various reformulations amongst a group and continuing in small groups.
- In a group of people who feel sufficiently at ease with each other, the reformulation can also be enacted; you can act a play about the problem situation, with the leading roles representing one of the subjects in the problem definition. The other participants can take inspiration from this and come up with new ideas.

30. FANTASTIC ANALOGY

Flow position: 6 and 7
Participants: 1 - 20
Requisites: pen, paper, marker pen, flip chart, possibly cartoon or book of fairy tales

Contrary to the natural analogy method (tool 28), based on existing, natural concepts, this method makes use of the world of fantasy. In it, the participants imagine situations which go beyond the bounds of reality. The fantastic opportunities that this offers are the source of inspiration for new potential solutions. The various methods by which this can be achieved are described below.

Method 1, the superhero

1. Have the participants imagine a hero or heroine from a book, movie, television program or similar.
2. Then have the participants imagine that they are this hero or heroine.
3. Confront these heroes (the participants) with the problem definition.
4. Have the participants as the heroes come up with 3 to 5 (impossible) solutions and write them down.
5. Collect up the solutions and generate new ideas within the entire group, inspired by these solutions.

Method 2, Tom & Jerry

1. In the group, watch a cartoon (video) with all sorts of impossible happenings (such as Tom & Jerry).
2. Have the participants each note down at least five impossible events.
3. Have each participant try to note down one (impossible) solution relating to the problem definition for each event noted down.
4. Collect up the solutions and generate new ideas within the entire group, inspired by these solutions.

Method 3, the fairy tale variation

As for method 2, but with a fairy tale read out loud or related instead of a movie.

Assignment

- Imagine a hero (heroine) and solve the following problem from his or her point of view:

  "How do I prevent myself from becoming too fat".
- Watch any cartoon movie and note how many impossible events happen in it.

The superhero

⇦A hero from our youth

- The fairy tale variation can also be used in a different way: read the story out (or tell it) up to the point where the main character is confronted with a problem. Stop telling the story and get the participants to each solve this problem in their own way in the manner of a fairy tale. Use these solutions to generate new ideas for the problem.

- If the fairy tale is well known, the participants can be asked to note down impossible happenings in the story without it being told. The advantages of this are: the ability to distance oneself from the problem properly by concentrating on the story, and a good incubation time. Ideas are generated using the impossible solutions that the participants have come up with as the source of inspiration.

- Just watching a cartoon can be a great source of inspiration! Use this to generate even more ideas.

Flow position: 6 and 7
Participants: 1 - 20
Requisites: pen, paper, marker pen, flip chart

Metaphors are expressions which have a figurative meaning.
Concepts are enhanced by the addition of a visual element,
usually very graphic. In doing so you paint a picture that
everyone can easily visualize (cold: cold as ice, strong: as strong
as an ox, camel: ship of the desert). By looking for a metaphor
for the problem definition or for a number of essential concepts
in it, a metaphorical reformulation can be created which enables
you to come up with a number of completely different solutions.
The art is naturally to translate these metaphorical solutions
back into good ideas relating to the original problem.

Method
1. Try to find a metaphor for the problem definition as a whole.
   In practice, this is usually best done by starting with the core
   concepts from the problem definition.
2. Decide which concepts in this reformulation are the most
   important.
3. Make a note of new ideas and potential solutions for these
   concepts in the reformulation.
4. Try to translate these ideas back into the original problem
   definition.
5. Note the new potential solutions and ideas that arise.

Example

A topical question which is often asked at UNHCR (UN refugee organization) is: "How can we get a good insight into the various streams of refugees in disaster and war areas?" A metaphor for this problem definition might be: "How does a biologist get a good insight into the activities of a colony of ants?"

Assignment

- Think of a number of obvious or less obvious metaphors for the concepts:
- Fat, free, necking, running, red.
- Find a metaphor for the sentence:
  'How can we increase production?'

Tips and tricks

- The following descriptions can be found in dictionaries:
⇨'use of word in figurative sense',

⇨'metaphor based on similarity',

⇨'figurative expression".

- By finding several metaphors for various concepts, the number of new ideas can be multiplied.
- When using this method, it is essential to clearly explain the term "metaphor". You can avoid problems in drawing up the metaphorical reformulation by giving a few examples and briefly practicing naming metaphors.

Flow position:	6 and 7
Participants:	1 - 20
Requisites:	pen, paper, marker pen, flip chart

This method is quite similar to the natural analogy method, but any possible connection with the problem definition is ruled out by making use of chance (except if chance plays its part and the random information is in fact very closely related to the problem!). By picking a word, picture or object completely at random, you can properly distance yourself from the problem. Starting with this word, picture or object, you can come up with a number of new potential solutions, either directly or indirectly. The random information is of course used as the source of inspiration and association.

Method
1. Pick a method to come up with random information (e.g. for a word: page 28, line 10, 3rd word of any random book).
2. Use this word, image or object to inspire you to come up with new ideas relating to the problem.
3. Repeat if necessary with other random information.

Assignment
- Think of a method for deciding on a random picture or object.
- Think of another method for deciding on a random word.

Tips and tricks

- This method is easy to implement and can easily be extended or combined with other methods.
- A flower or chain association (tools 15 and 16) based on the random information can directly supply a large number of inspiring words and/or pictures.
- A forced chain association from the random information back to the core concept of the problem definition guides your thoughts slowly back to the problem, each step being a potential source of information.
- Because this method is so simple it is also easy to implement in large groups, by working on the same problem in small groups but with different random information. It is then important to discuss all the ideas with the whole group afterwards.

Flow position:	6 and 7
Participants:	2 - 20
Requisites:	pen, paper, marker pen, flip chart

The morphological box is a method specifically intended to find alternatives based on the characteristics of a concept, and thus develop new ideas. It consists of a structured, analytical part and a specific, creative part. In it, randomly chosen alternative characteristics are coupled with a new, as yet non-existent whole. This is then used as the source of inspiration for new ideas.

Method

1. Pick out the most characteristic concept from the problem definition.
2. Make a list of the essential characteristics of the concept you have chosen.
3. Make a table with the characteristics found in 2. above along the vertical axis, and alternatives 1 to x along the horizontal axis.
4. Enter x number of alternatives in the table for each characteristic found, and make a note of them; you now have a morphological box.
5. Make a combination of alternatives that have nothing to do with one another (one from each characteristic) and try to come up with new ideas with the new thing that has come into being in this way.

Characte-ristic	Step	Altern. 1	Altern. 2	Altern. 3	Altern. 4
steering	joy stick	steering wheel	banking	rudder	track-guided
Porter	baggage carrier	luggage trolley	trailer	overhead rail	bin
mobility	wheels	caterpillars	monorail	skis	hovercraft
drive	leg power	gas motor	wind	solar energy	battery
position of manager	standing	sitting	lying	suspended	no manager

Example for one step.

Assignment

Make a morphological box for the expression "refrigerator" and think of alternatives for a refrigerator using this morphological box.

Tips and tricks

- This method is particularly useful for product development in a technical environment. It forces the participants to think about and to work with different possible and impossible alternatives.
- The more characteristics and alternatives you put down, the bigger the morphological box becomes. The bigger the morphological box, the greater the number of creativity-inspiring possibilities.
- An extra dimension can be added by also getting the participants to draw the selected combination of alternative characteristics (see method, step 5),.

Flow position:	6 and 7
Participants:	4 - 20
Requisites:	pen, paper, marker pen, flip chart

Matec stands for **Mat**rice d'**E**loignement **C**reatif, a creative distancing table. It is a structural method of arriving at a number of words which can then be used as the basis for the natural analogy method. By working in this way, the whole group can be distanced from the problem through games and at the same time get practice in associating.

Method

1. Pick 3 core concepts from the problem definition that can be visualized.
2. Take the first term and note down on the horizontal axis the first 5 words of a chain association which you have done collectively.
3. With the group, make five new chain associations based on these five words, which you will then write down vertically underneath.
4. Make the same sort of table with the two core expressions left over.
5. Choose a number of expressions which are a long way removed from the problem from the three matrices and use these in the natural analogy method.

stairs →	tree →	beer →	drink →	water
↓	↓	↓	↓	↓
kick	step	stomach	alcohol	Ice
↓	↓	↓	↓	↓
earth	pro-gress	body	control	fridge
↓	↓	↓	↓	↓
garden	speed	pension	police	kitchen
↓	↓	↓	↓	↓
pond	danger	money	cap	eating

Assignment

Make a MATEC table with "PC" as the starting word.

Tips and tricks

- In addition to forming the basis for the natural analogy method, MATEC is also a fun activity in itself and is good practice for learning to associate. It is also ideal as a warm-up at the beginning of the creativity session and as a means of getting a group to get to know one another.
- Make sure that everyone sticks to making chain associations and not flower associations.
- Try not to take too long making the matrices, but also ensure that everybody gets a turn; if necessary, go through the participants in turn.

Flow position: 6 and 7
Participants: 2 - 20
Requisites: pen, paper, marker pen, flip chart

In this method, the participants are put to work themselves. They are asked to make collages about various scenes using pictures and texts from newspapers, thus creating a number of pictures which will provide the source of inspiration for new ideas. The use of pictures gives an additional dimension to the task, which can be expanded even further by allowing the participants to draw things in themselves.

Method

1. Pick any number of themes based on or to do with the problem definition and distribute these amongst a similar number of groups.
2. Provide newspapers, scissors and glue and have the groups put together a collage to do with their topic by sticking pictures and text together.
3. Discuss the results with the whole group and if necessary, ask the various groups to explain their collages.
4. Hang each collage up in turn and allow new ideas relating to the original problem definition to come to the fore, inspired by the pictures.

Assignment

Make a note of a number of topics which can be used with this method to make collages for the problem: "What should the bathroom of the future look like?"

Tips and tricks

- Tell the participants that they should note down any ideas that they have while they are cutting and pasting so that they do not forget them later.
- Keep the time allocated to making the collages short; exerting a slight pressure makes for rapid choices and gives all sorts of associations more chance.
- When explaining the collages, allow any additions to be drawn or written in so that ideas are lost.

Flow position:	6 and 7
Participants:	1 - 20
Requisites:	pen, paper, marker pen, flip chart

Poetic stimulation is a way of getting the participants in a creativity session intensively involved with words, pictures and language. By choosing a number of core concepts or themes from the problem and using these to produce a haiku or a limerick, you can reveal angles that could lead to new ideas. Depending on how the group leader assesses the group, he or she will have to choose one of the two totally different poetic forms (see also the explanation of these poetic forms).

Method
1. Pick one or more core concepts or themes from (or to do with) the problem definition.
2. Explain what a haiku or limerick entails and what the background and objective of these poetic forms are (choose one of them or let the participants make the choice).
3. Have the participants write one or more texts using the themes chosen.
4. Read the texts one at a time and institute a new round of ideas for each text (linking back to the original problem).

Example

The limerick is a form of rhyme that has strict rules concerning the form and rhythm of the text. It is built up as follows:

Line 1: 8 or 9 syllables

Line 2: 8 or 9 syllables rhyming with line 1

Line 3: 5 syllables

Line 4: 5 syllables rhyming with line 3

Line 5: 8 or 9 syllables rhyming with line 1 and line 2.

> **There was a young lady from Kent,**
>
> **Who said that she knew what it meant.**
>
> **When men asked her to dine,**
>
> **Gave her gin, rum and wine.**
>
> **She knew what it meant but she went.**

The haiku is a poetic form of Japanese origin. It consists of 3 lines with a total of 17 syllables. The first line consists of 5 syllables, the second of 7 and the third line of 5. It is very important that the verse expresses a feeling of empathy (with nature). A haiku is often compiled around an (apparent) contradiction in the various sentences.

> **Blackbird builds a nest**
> **of many dry, dead branches**
> **New life is born**

Assignment

- Try to write a haiku yourself that meets the above requirements.
- Do the same with a limerick. Pick a theme yourself.

Tips and tricks

- The haiku and the limerick are totally different poetic forms. It is also very important to think carefully about the capabilities of the group before choosing which form to use. The haiku relies a lot more on content and imagination whilst the limerick relies more on form and rhythm.
- It is sometimes helpful to hang a description of the haiku and the limerick on the wall so that it can be referred to during the course of the work.

37. PROVOCATIVE SUB-DIVISION

Flow position:	6 and 7
Participants:	1 - 20
Requisites:	pen, paper, marker pen, flip chart

The provocative sub-division tool is intended to enable you to gradually distance yourself from the problem. The method is based on a process of sub-dividing the problem even further into core concepts and derived terms, which then enable you to come up with other angles on the problem. Provocative or illogical sub-division makes it much easier to eliminate the problem.

Method
1. Pick a crucial term from the problem.
2. Divide this term into two concepts.
3. Generate new ideas from this sub-division.
4. Divide these two concepts into provocative concepts derived from them.
5. Generate new concepts, ideas and potential solutions from these.
6. Repeat steps 4 and 5 as long as necessary, always working from the derived concepts.

Example 109

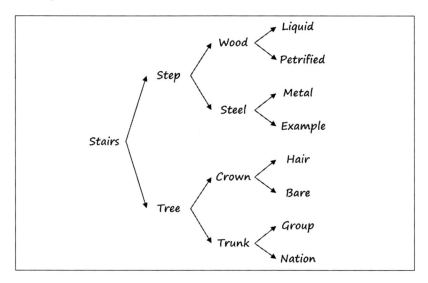

Assignment

- Make sub-divisions in 3 steps with "file" as the starting word.
- Make 3 provocative sub-divisions of the concept "freeway".

Tips and tricks

- Indicate clearly what logical, content-based sub-divisions are, for example "inside and outside", "front and back", "form and function". You can then explain the provocative sub-divisions; all sub-divisions that provoke, that bring about the elimination of the problem.
- A logical sub-division of the letters of the relevant word can also be used as a starting point, for example "freeway" sub-divided into "free" and "way" (or even into "few" and "year").
- What here is logical and what is provocative, or does that not actually apply?

38. PROVOCATIVE QUESTIONING

Flow position: 6 and 7
Participants: 1 - 20
Requisites: pen, paper, marker pen, flip chart

In this method you use questions which require the participants to take another look at the problem. An aid to this is the so-called Osborn checklist, consisting of nine compulsory changes to the problem definition with a view to generating new potential solutions.

Osborn's checklist:

Imagine if we were to .....

1. change it
2. enlarge it
3. make it smaller
4. adapt it
5. rearrange it
6. turn it around
7. replace it
8. use it another way
9. combine it   ..... what would happen then?

Method
1. Pick a crucial term from the problem that can be visualized (drawn).
2. Apply one or more questions from Osborn's checklist to it.
3. Generate ideas based on this new suggestion.

4. Repeat the procedure as necessary using other provocative
   questions.

Example

Assignment
- Note down the thoughts that are generated when questions 2, 6 and 8 from the checklist are applied to the "fruit dish" concept.
- Think of new products for a manufacturer of camping tents using questions 3, 5 and 9.

Tips and tricks
- To explain this method and to illustrate its effect (alienation), you can use close-up photographs of objects which make them not immediately recognizable. The use of objects for purposes other than those for which they were intended can clarify the function of asking the questions.
- It is a good idea to hang Osborn's checklist on the wall when using this method.

39. DESIGN METHOD

Flow position: 6 and 7
Participants: 1 - 20
Requisites: pen, paper, marker pen, flip chart

This method is actually a visual form of the search for presuppositions. By not writing the ideas down but by sketching them out you can give other aspects of ideas a chance. The visual senses also get additional stimulation. By filtering the presuppositions from the pictures you have collected more and more new opportunities are opened up.

Method
1. Have the participants sketch out at least one spontaneous solution.
2. Note down the characteristics which these sketches have in common.
3. Have the participants sketch out new ideas which do not have the collective characteristics noted down.
4. Take another look at all the sketches and note down again the characteristics which they have in common.
5. Repeat from 3. as long as necessary or possible.

Assignment
1. Decide for yourself what type of problem this method would be suitable for.
2. Try to sketch out the above-mentioned assignment of sketching out solutions.

Tips and tricks

- The game Pictionary can be played as a good warm-up when using this method. This can get rid of any hesitation there may be with regard to drawing.
- After a few drawing rounds you can of course always continue verbally. Whichever way you choose to operate, hang the sketches on the wall or circulate them amongst the participants to use as a source of inspiration.

40. CLUSTERING

Flow position:	9
Participants:	1 - 20
Requisites:	marker pen, flip chart, Post-it® notes, cards

Clustering is putting the ideas you have come up with into an initial order, or subdividing them into "clusters". This gives the group and/or yourself a clearer picture of the ideas that have been put forward.

A disadvantage perhaps is that the choice of clusters once again forces you to follow patterns.

Method

The following points are important when clustering ideas:

- Similar and identical ideas are brought together in blocks.
- Begin a new block, a cluster, with an idea that does not fit in with the other ideas.
- Give all clusters a name; there will usually be one cluster called "Miscellaneous".
- Ideas can be placed in several clusters.

Example  115

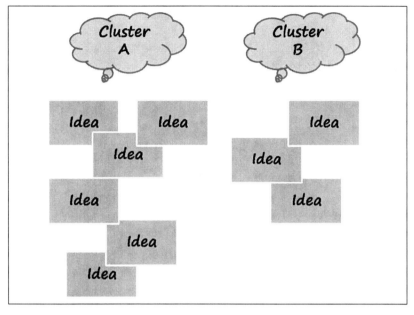

Tips and tricks

- Use cards or Post-it® notes when brainstorming. This will make clustering simpler.
- Clustering is often used as the first step in a selection process. Some ideas can be combined and dealt with as one idea. Some clusters can perhaps be done away with.

Flow position: 9
Participants: 1 - 20
Requisites: pen, paper, marker pen, flip chart, 🖳

Solutions must satisfy the criteria specified by the problem
owner. Criteria can vary according to the problem context.
Possible criteria are:

- available budget,
- time frame,
- technical feasibility,
- attention to environmental aspects.

Criteria can be determined on the basis of requirements and
wishes. The former must always be met (either yes or no): the
latter can be met on a gradual basis.

Method

1. Give the ideas that remain a ranking number (or retain the
   original numbering).
2. Set the selected ideas against the criteria established in a
   criteria list.
3. Fill in the list with
   - words (yes, no, seldom, etc.)
   - numbers (example "scale number")
   - symbols (📑, ●, ▶ , 🖳 etc.)
4. Note a conclusion for each idea.

The results can form a further basis for idea development.

Example   117

	Idea's			
Criteria	1	2	3	4
Budget		🝙	🝙	
Time frame		🕛		
Environment		♻	♻	
etcetera				
Conclusion		🙂		

Tips and tricks

Paper too small? Put the ideas in the vertical axis and the criteria in the horizontal axis.

42. HITS

Flow position: 9
Participants: 1 - 20
Requisites: pen, paper, marker pen, flip chart,
                      adhesive dots

Indicating hits is a method of making an initial positive selection
by indicating the most promising ideas with a dot or similar.
(Scrapping poor ideas would be a negative selection). The "hits"
technique thus puts a collection of ideas into a manageable
from.

Method
1. Give everyone a number of dots (the number of hits can vary,
   for example seven for each participant, three per cluster or as
   many as you like).
2. Think it over first and then place the dots. You should do this
   together if possible in order to prevent others influencing
   your opinion.

Example 119

Hits	Ideas
■■	Twitter
■	By DVD
■■■■	Ning
■■■	Our website

Tips and tricks

After scoring the hits the most interesting ideas can be mapped out using the "low hanging fruits" technique (tool 7).

43. WRA

Flow position:	9
Participants:	1 - 10
Requisites:	pen, paper, marker pen, flip chart

The letters W, R and A stand for wastepaper bin, refrigerator and agenda. This method is intended to evaluate a number of ideas, a distinction being made between the ideas that can be thrown away (wastepaper bin), ideas that need to be put on ice (refrigerator) and ideas which can be worked on immediately (agenda). The group instinctively makes a choice from a large number of ideas.

Method
1. Put together a list of ideas that can be assessed in this way.
2. Let each participant categorize the ideas into W, R and A him or herself.
3. Collect the results and put them in a table on a big piece of paper.
4. On the basis of the results, determine with the group which ideas should definitely be placed on the agenda (i.e. what the group should take further).

Example   121

Ideas	Waste-paper bin	Fridge	Agenda	Choice yes/no
1				
2				
3				
4				
...				
...				

Tips and tricks

- Use a standard table on A4 paper. This can be used by participants to make their own categories.
- Make sure that the list of ideas to be assessed is not too big to fit onto one A4 side. Otherwise it will take too much time and effort to assess them.

MIND TWISTER

Two dots

Draw two dots on a piece of paper and than join them together.

Solution: usually people join the two dots with a straight line, sometimes with a curved one. It is only rarely that anyone thinks of folding the paper over so that the two points are touching each other (breaking through paradigmatic thinking).

44. RESISTANCE TABLE

Flow position: 9
Participants: 1 - 20
Requisites: pen, paper, marker pen, flip chart

This method is intended to look at selected ideas in a critical way, with the focus on any resistance there may be from the company or organization. By listing which groups or people will present a lot of or little resistance to each idea, we can look for the best solutions. You can examine why this resistance has occurred and what you can do about it.

Method
1. Make a table as shown below.
2. List which groups or people have something to do with or something to gain from the idea concerned.
3. With the participants, estimate how much resistance or agreement can be expected from these groups or people. Do this with the help of ++ (agreement, active cooperation), + (agreement, passive cooperation), 0 (neutral), - (resistance, passive opposition), -- (resistance, active opposition).
4. Using the chart, generate ideas to reduce the amount of opposition.
5. Select the solution/solutions that would ultimately be best accepted by the organization.

Example 123

Idea	Group/ person 1	Group/ person 2	Group/ person 3	Group/ person 4
1	+	++	--	0
2	0	-	+	-
3	++	0	+	+
4	--	-	0	+

Assignment

Choose a vacation destination for a group of friends and try to determine the amount of agreement or resistance with the help of the table.

Tips and tricks

- For an even better assessment you would also have to estimate the degree of influence of the various groups or persons. If you are in a position to do so you can incorporate a weighting factor in the graphic and thus make an even clearer priority list of resistance to be eliminated.

- Determining the level of influence can also be a factor in estimating whose resistance would be overruled by agreement/active cooperation. This is in fact a risky task, because this could reduce the commitment within the company or organization.

45. INFLUENCE ANALYSIS

Flow position: 9
Participants: 4 - 10
Requisites: pen, paper, marker pen, flip chart

The influence analysis lists the positive and negative points of an idea or plan so that these can be compared. It stimulates you to think about all aspects of the idea or plan and helps to find the consensus on the priorities of the factors on the left and right of the table. The influence analysis also follows up on its look at the real evaluation of the problem and the solution found.

Method
1. Write down the theme at the top of a table with two columns.
2. Write all supporting factors for an idea in the left-hand column and all opposing influences in the right-hand column (brainstorming!).
3. Give all the factors a score (e.g. 1-10).
4. Have a look at which supporting influences can be reinforced.
5. Determine which opposing influences can be limited (transformed into a supporting factor?).
6. Try to reach consensus, for example by means of discussion.

Example

Plan: Factory modernization with a new machine park		
Supportive	**Opposing**	
8 Customers want new products	⊃ ⊂ Loss of overtime for personnel	6
4 Increase productivity	⊃ ⊂ Afraid of new technology	6
6 Increase output volume	⊃ ⊂ Influence of new technology	2
1 Reduce maintenance costs	⊃ ⊂ Costs	6
	⊂ Disruption	2

Tips and tricks

Merely reinforcing the positive factors can have a contradictory effect, i.e. active opposition. It is often better to remove barriers.

46. PMI

Flow position:	9
Participants:	1 - 20
Requisites:	pen, paper, marker pen, flip chart, ⌨

PMI stands for plus/minus/interesting. Edward De Bono developed PMI as an instrument for considering ideas in more detail, thus facilitating decisionmaking. Possible applications also include the evaluation of a project, training course etc.

Method
1. Put the possible ideas in a table with 4 columns: alternatives, pluses (P), minuses (M) and interesting points (I).
2. For each alternative first think of all the positive points and benefits and then any possible negative points and disadvantages. Arguments that come to the fore during discussions but are not easy to place under either plusses or minuses should be placed under interesting points. For example, take three minutes for the advantages and three minutes for the disadvantages of each alternative.
3. Choose the best solution after considering all the points.

Example   127

Alternatives	Plus (P)	Minus (M)	Interesting (I)
Vacation in France	•Climate •Wine	•Busy during the high season	
Vacation in Norway	•Beauty of scenery •Relative few tourists	•More expensive •Long car journey	•Never been there before

Things can be taken from the interesting aspects which will make the idea interesting in other places.

47. NAA

Flow position: 9
Participants: 1 - 20
Requisites: pen, paper, marker pen, flip chart

The letters NAA in the name of this method stand for New, Attractive and Achievable. These are the criteria against which the ideas will be assessed. This method is mainly suitable for solving practical (technical) problems, but with a little creativity it can be used for solving other problems as well. It is important that the whole group reaches agreement over the assessment.

Method
1. Select the ideas to be tested against the criteria.
2. Make a table with the ideas in the vertical axis and the three criteria in the horizontal axis.
3. Determine with the group how the assessments are going to be indicated (e.g. with a +, 0, -, or with a scale number).
4. Fill in the table with the group. Make sure that there is agreement with regard to each assessment.
5. Determine the order of the ideas using the results in the table.

Example 129

Order established	Idea	New	Attractive	Achievable
	1			
	2			
	3			
	4			

Assignment

Describe the concepts "New", "Attractive" and "Achievable".

Tips and tricks

- Before you apply this method try to determine with the group how you are going to use the concepts new, attractive and achievable. The best way is to get a collective definition of the concepts which you then hang on the wall as a reminder.
- If you know that this method is going to be suitable, you can make the table in advance so that you only need to fill it in during the session.

48. ELIMINATION RACE

Flow position: 9
Participants: 1 - 20
Requisites: pen, paper, marker pen, flip chart

Comparison of your ideas in pairs, also known as the elimination race, entails making an (initial) selection of the ideas. A disadvantage is that ideas which have been rejected in this way may still be some of the best.

Method
Compare two ideas at a time and determine which is the best. Continue with this until you have an acceptable number left.

Flow position:	9 and 10
Participants:	1 - 20
Requisites:	marker pen, flip chart

The solution resistance table enables you to map out the resistance to ideas and to formulate answers.

Method

1. Collect the ideas using the clustering method (tool 40) and/or hits scoring method (tool 42).
2. Sort the suggestions on the left-hand side of the solution resistance table into different solution groups, putting comparable suggestions next to each other and different suggestions underneath each other. Then sort the ideas within the groups - from general to solution details (see example).
3. In order to arrive at practical solutions, ask whether each suggestion will encounter resistance or what negative consequences are to be expected ("who or what will be against it?"). Mark the suggestions to which resistance is expected. Note down the resistance on the right-hand side of the solution resistance table. Then alter the relevant suggestion, until all resistance has been removed.
4. In order to arrive at the solution to be implemented in the first instance you can compare several solutions in a solution overview. Think about:
⇨what measures can be applied without investment?
⇨what measures can be implemented without consequent

costs?

⇨ what measures carry with them extra risks?

⇨ what measures need to be reversed if necessary?

⇨ what measures fit in with the business or departmental objectives?

Example

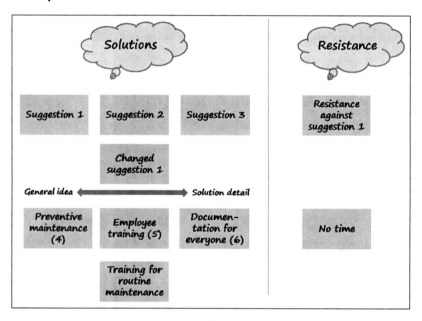

Tips and tricks

If there are different ways of eliminating a problem, evaluate them according to effort, yield and own influence using the "low hanging fruits" method (tool 7).

Flow position:	9 and 10
Participants:	1 - 20
Requisites:	pen, paper, marker pen, flip chart, stickers, Post-it® notes

Are the bad ideas really so bad or are they good? Perhaps they have interesting aspects upon closer inspection. Play the angel's advocate and see whether there is not something which could be retrieved from them. Conversely, why not try playing the devil's advocate and stomp the best ideas into the ground.

Example

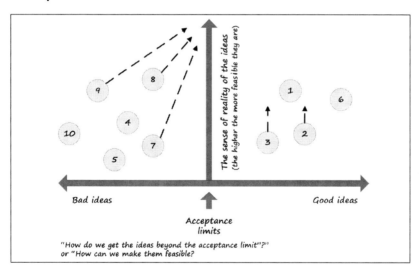

"How do we get the ideas beyond the acceptance limit" or "how can we make them feasible?"

Method

1. When selecting the ideas, give each participant three stickers for determining the best ideas, plus one sticker in a different color for marking the worst idea. One of the participants temporarily plays the role of the advocate for each idea.

2. If you are the:

   a) <u>angel's advocate:</u>

   Ask why the bad ideas are not good and try to improve them.

   b) <u>devil's advocate:</u>

   Ask what is not good about the good ideas.

Tips and tricks

The PMI method (tool 46) can be used as an aid for working things out in greater detail.

51. PLAN OF ACTION

Flow position:	10
Participants:	1 - 20
Requisites:	pen, paper, marker pen, flip chart, 🖥

A plan of action is a summary of everything that you have to do in order to implement a solution. With a plan of action you promote the systematic implementation of measures. A plan of action generates a script which you can use to go through everything that has to be done. You can also use it as a basis for issuing other information to other people. Once it has been completed the plan of action should be used as a guideline for implementation.

Method
The plan of action can be set up in the following way:

1. Sub-divide the actions and the objective that has been set over a number of steps.
2. Draw up a time frame and a cost calculation for each step.
3. Add any missing steps to the plan of action.
4. Set a completion date and arrange the division of tasks for each action.
5. Draw up the plan of action by summarizing the decisions in table form (see example).
6. Make sure that there is a commitment for the plan of action.

Nr.	Actions	Requirements	Employee responsible	Date	Completion date	Status/ comments

Project: ...   Date: ...   Page: ... from...
Team: ...

Assignment

In two weeks you have to arrange a presentation on the creative thinking process for a number of managers. You will have to deal with the invitations, reserve the room, provide the overhead projector, the flip chart, make overheads and map out the target group and the objectives etc. Draw up a plan of action.

Tips and tricks

Every plan of action looks different. The following questions will help you to draw one up:

- What is the problem?
- What actions have to be undertaken to implement it (e.g. writing guidelines, creating training opportunities, obtaining approval)?
- Who carries the responsibility for each separate action point (organization)?
- When are these action points implemented?

- Where are the action points implemented?
- How much time does it take to implement an action point?
- How is the success of an action point established?
- What is the budget?
- What are the quality criteria?
- Who gets what information?

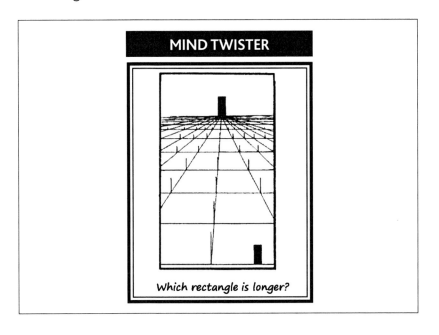

Books

Jan-Willem van de Brandhof
The Business Brain Book
Brainware 2008 ISBN 978-90-812883-1-6

Igor Byttebier & Ramon Vullings
Creativity Today
BIS Publishers 2007 ISBN 978-90-6369-146-2

Nancy Margulies
Mapping Inner Space
Zephyr Press 2002 ISBN 1-56976-138-8

Jamie Nast
Idea Mapping
Wiley 2006 ISBN 978-0-471-78862-1

Tony Davila, Marc J. Epstein & Robert Shelton
Making Innovation Work
Wharton 2006 ISBN 0-13-149786-3

Software

Thought Office
Innovation Software
http://www.thoughtoffice.com/

Visualizing and organizing ideas

http://www.inspiration.com/

Mind Mapping
MindManager, iMindMap, FreeMind, XMind, DropMind,
ConceptDraw, MindMeister, NovaMind and others.

Organizations
CreaMatics
www.creamatics.nl

Leo Groote Institute
http://www.leogroote.nl/

World of Minds
www.worldofminds.com

Hypershifters
www.hypershifters.com

New and Improved
http://www.newandimproved.com/

Innovation Tools
http://www.innovationtools.com/

FacilitatorU
http://www.facilitatoru.com/

On the authors:

Max van Leeuwen has more than twenty solid years exposure in the field of creativity. He is most experienced in working with groups to create ideas and commitments. He works with entrepreneurs and their employees, management teams and other groups in organisations to solve problems or to fulfil wishes. He uses most of the techniques explained in this book and also, thorough research and experimentation, variations or new forms and methods. Main issue in his way of working is to start with the problem given and to end with action, what are we going to do to solve it.

See LinkedIn for more information of Max van Leeuwen

Hans Terhurne is a seasoned trainer and facilitator for more than 30 years. He is fascinated by using the brain better in business environments, an approach which utilizes brain capacities through visual mapping. His goal is to help his clients (individuals and groups on management and employee level) to solve organizational items by using creativity tools and especially through visual mapping techniques. Our brains are very good at absorbing processing and remembering information in a visual form, reason why Hans always is looking for new visual thinking applications to solve client issues.

See LinkedIn for more information of Hans Terhurne.

CPSIA information can be obtained at www.ICGtesting.com
Printed in the USA
LVOW032217121211

259124LV00006B/89/P